HISTORY OF FUN STUFF

The Sweet Story of Hot Chocolate!

by Stephen Krensky
illustrated by Rob McClurkan

Ready-to-Read

Simon Spotlight
New York   London   Toronto   Sydney   New Delhi

SIMON SPOTLIGHT

An imprint of Simon & Schuster Children's Publishing Division

1230 Avenue of the Americas, New York, New York 10020

This Simon Spotlight edition October 2014

Text copyright © 2014 by Simon & Schuster, Inc.

Illustrations copyright © 2014 by Rob McClurkan

For information about special discounts for bulk purchases, please contact

Simon & Schuster Special Sales at 1-866-506-1949 or business@simonandschuster.com.

Manufactured in the United States of America 1014 LAK

2 4 6 8 10 9 7 5 3

Library of Congress Cataloging-in-Publication Data

The sweet story of hot chocolate! / Stephen Krensky ; illustrated by Rob McClurkan.

pages cm — (History of fun stuff)

Audience: Age 6 to 8. Audience: Grades K to 3.

1. Chocolate drinks—History—Juvenile literature. I. Title.

TX817.C4K74 2014   641.3'374—dc23   2014009883

ISBN 978-1-4814-2052-5 (pbk)

ISBN 978-1-4814-2053-2 (hc)

ISBN 978-1-4814-2054-9 (eBook)

CONTENTS

CHAPTER 1
A Special Drink

On a cold winter morning, a cup of
hot chocolate hits the spot. That goes
for winter afternoons, too. And winter
evenings. Or any time there's a little
chill in the air. All by itself, or topped
with marshmallows or whipped cream,
hot chocolate is hard to beat.

But do you know who drank hot chocolate first? And how they made it? Or how long it took to become popular around the world? Or what was the strangest thing ever added to it? (Hint: It has to do with whales, but more on that later.)

That's where this book comes in. By the time you finish reading it, you'll know the answers to all these questions and many more. You will be a History of Fun Stuff Expert on hot chocolate!

Hot chocolate begins as a bean that grows in a pod on the cacao [ka-KOW] tree. The word *cacao* looks familiar, right? That's because the English word *cocoa* comes from the word *cacao*. After the beans are dried and roasted, the shells are removed. What's left is called the nibs. They are crushed into small bits or a fine powder. So far that sounds simple enough. But how long do you think this has been going on?

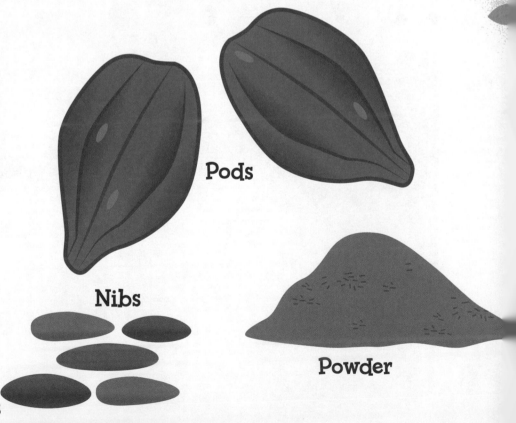

Pods

Nibs

Powder

Records show that the Olmec people of Central America were growing cacao beans at least 3,500 years ago (2,700 years before anyone started roasting another kind of bean to make coffee).

The cacao beans became especially popular once somebody decided (and convinced other people) that they had magical properties when ground up and mixed with water and different ingredients, like chiles, corn, or honey, to name a few. They used this drink as a medicine, as well as something to have on special occasions.

As time went on, knowledge of the drink was passed from the Olmecs to the Mayans, and then to the Aztecs. The cacao beans were even used as a kind of money. With only one bean you could get yourself a tamale. But if you were planning

a big dinner with friends or family, you could trade a hundred beans for a turkey. Of course you would need more beans than that if you planned on serving hot chocolate during the meal.

CHAPTER 2
Hot Chocolate Makes a Splash

Once Columbus visited the New World, cacao beans soon became known abroad. The conquistadors [kan-KEES-ta-doors] from Spain learned about the Aztecs' chocolate drink as they swept through the future Mexico. One leader, Hernán Cortés,

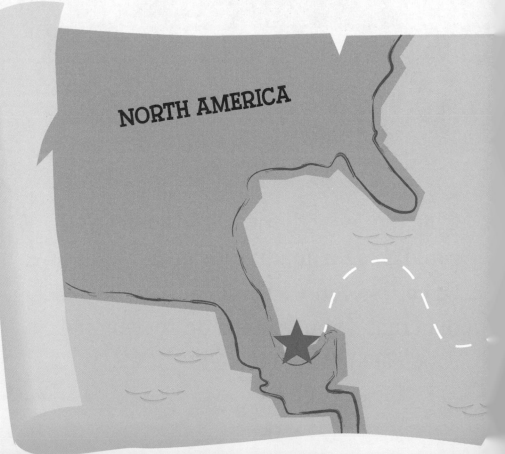

NORTH AMERICA

brought it back to the Spanish court in the 1520s. There was just one problem. The Spanish thought the drink tasted awful. But all was not lost. The royal chefs experimented with new ingredients. They tried adding sugar and cinnamon among other ingredients to make the drink taste sweeter. And was all that experimenting a success?

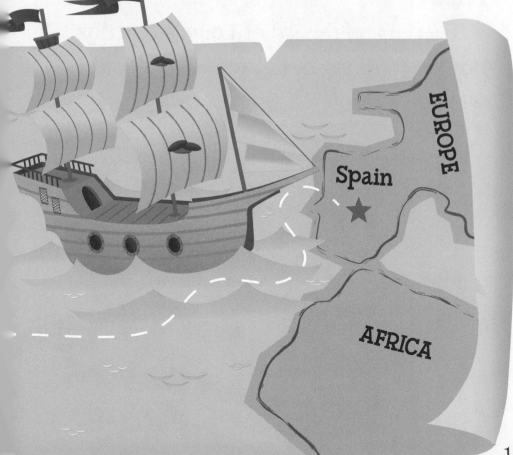

It certainly was. In fact, the Spanish liked their chocolate so much they didn't trade it for a hundred years. But it was hard for them to keep the drink a secret forever, especially with marriages between royalty and an increase in travel. There is a story, for example, that Spanish princess Maria Theresa sent a chest full of chocolate to her fiancée, King Louis XIV of France.

There is no record of Louis's reaction, but the wedding definitely went ahead as planned in 1660.

The new drink was very popular in France, and soon made the jump across the English Channel. Around the same time, the British conquered the Caribbean island of Jamaica. Jamaica had tropical weather and sandy beaches, and cacao beans grew there.

That meant the British had their own source of necessary ingredients.

Hot chocolate's popularity spurred the creation of chocolate houses, places where people could gather to drink and talk. The first one opened in London in 1657.

The British colonists in America also knew a good drink when they found one. During the Revolutionary War, soldiers in the Continental Army received more than musket balls for signing up. They also received a monthly ration of chocolate in the form of a small cake.

The soldiers would cut off thin pieces from the cake and put them in boiling water. The army had a reputation for not having enough food and clothing for its men, but at least the soldiers always had hot chocolate to console themselves.

The taste for hot chocolate extended all the way up the chain of command. George Washington enjoyed what he called chocolate cream, and he was not the only Founding Father who did so. Thomas Jefferson loved hot chocolate too. He even thought it would become more popular than tea or coffee. He may not have been right about that, but Jefferson was a well-known admirer of good food and drink, and so his opinion helped spread the word.

CHAPTER 3
Tinkering with Success

A lot of people probably thought hot chocolate couldn't get any better. After all, for thousands of years the recipe had simply called for cacao nibs ground into bits or powder and added to hot water (and later, milk) along with other flavors. But a Dutch chemist wondered if improvements could still be made. In 1828 a process emerged to separate cocoa butter from the nibs.

The remaining powder, called Dutch cocoa or cocoa powder, was easier to make drinks with because it dissolved more easily into milk or water. Hot cocoa, slightly different from hot chocolate, was born.

Among those who later bought one of these machines were the sons of John Cadbury of England, who were developing chocolate products of their own. Cadbury chocolates are still being produced today. Have you ever tried one of them?

Chicago World's Fair

1893

Come See

Chocolate Manufacturing Machines

In 1847 the British chocolate company J.S. Fry & Sons began mixing Dutch cocoa with melted cocoa butter. The result was a sweet paste that could be molded into chocolate bars. This was the first time that chocolate was eaten as a solid food instead of only being used as an ingredient in the hot chocolate drink. Not

surprisingly, it was popular at once. Some
of the chocolate-manufacturing machines
were exhibited at the Chicago World's Fair
in 1893. After the fair ended, they were
bought by an enterprising candy maker
named Milton Hershey. Have you ever
heard his name before?

Hershey first used the chocolate from his new machines to coat the caramel he'd already made. But then he sold that company to start a new venture.

He bought a large tract of farmland in Pennsylvania. He needed the land to build a factory where cows would graze nearby. Why cows? Because Hershey wanted to manufacture bars of milk chocolate, which until then were an expensive treat. To do that, of course, he would need a lot of milk.

It took Hershey a while to develop the right formula. His first chocolate bars appeared in 1900 and have been a big success ever since. Even today, some people like to break off a piece of a Hershey's chocolate bar and melt it into a cup of hot chocolate to make it sweeter.

CHAPTER 4
Hot Chocolate on the Move

Even though hot chocolate originated in warm climates, it has a special appeal on a cold day. And the days don't get much colder than the ones at the North and South Poles. When Norwegian explorer Roald Amundsen was looking for the South Pole in 1911, he made sure everyone in his expedition was well supplied with chocolate. It helped keep up everyone's strength as the group crossed the frozen landscape. And maybe it even helped him to become the first person to reach the South Pole on December 14 of that year.

Hot cocoa also continued to be a favorite of American soldiers. It was included in combat rations during World War II and is still a staple of military cuisine.

Today's troops are issued Meals, Ready to Eat (MREs) featuring such taste-bud teasers as beef teriyaki and chicken fajitas. But they also include cocoa mix in case the soldiers are in the mood for some quick energy and a reliable taste of home.

Of course for some people, drinking hot chocolate isn't complete without a few marshmallows sitting on top. Originally marshmallows were made from egg whites, sugar, and the sap of the marshmallow plant, which is where they got their name. In the 1800s, French candy makers started substituting gelatin for the marshmallow sap. They kept the name, though, maybe because it sounded better than anything new they could come up with, even in French. Today's marshmallows are run through machines that mold the mixture into soft cubes with rounded corners.

They are available in both large and small sizes, and will melt in a cup of hot chocolate after first floating on the top. But are marshmallows the only thing people put in hot chocolate?

Certainly not. Let's not forget about whipped cream. Like butter and regular cream, whipped cream starts out as milk. Records of its popularity date to the 1500s. To create it, cream that had risen to the top of the milk was gently whipped to create foam that could be taken away. The whipping had to be done carefully, though. If it was done too strenuously, the cream would turn to butter. The foam was then sweetened with sugar. Sometimes known as snow cream, whipped cream took a while to create by hand. By the late 1800s, making whipped cream became much easier with the invention of machines that separated the cream mechanically.

These days, hot chocolate is a drink enjoyed around the world. Not that everyone enjoys it in exactly the same way. In Morocco, hot chocolate is flavored with orange and spice. In Austria, the whipped cream piled on top may be just as important as the hot chocolate hidden underneath. In Mexico, vanilla

and cinnamon are favored flavors. The strangest thing ever added to hot chocolate, though, is probably ambergris. This is a kind of fat that lines the intestines of sperm whales. A 19th century French food writer recommended adding it to chocolate drinks. What do you think of that idea?

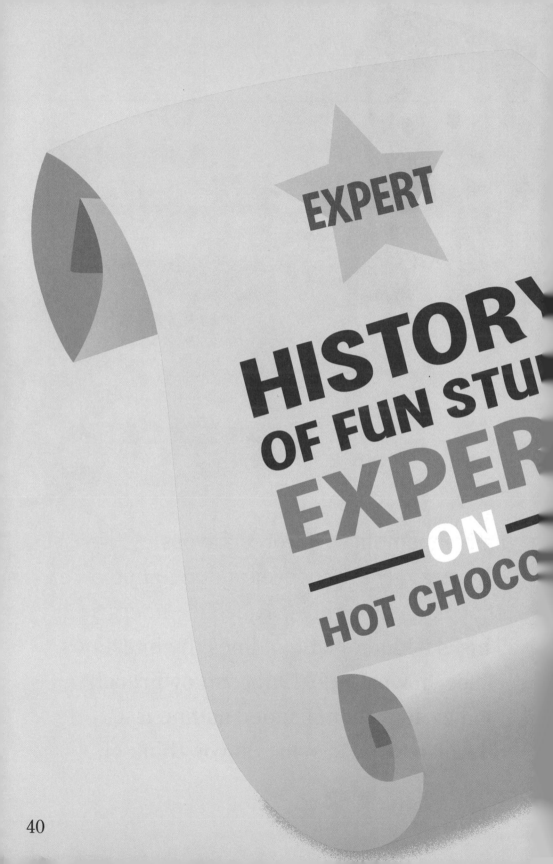

EXPERT

HISTORY
OF FUN STU
EXPER
ON
HOT CHOCO

Congratulations! You've come to the end of this book. You are now an official History of Fun Stuff Expert on hot chocolate. Go ahead and impress your friends and family with all the cool stuff you've learned about one of the world's most popular drinks. And don't forget to enjoy a delicious cup of hot chocolate as soon as possible!

EXPERT

Hey, kids! Now that you're an expert on the history of hot chocolate, turn the page to learn even more about this tasty treat, plus some science, geography, and history of money along the way!

The Layers of the Tropical Rain Forest

Chocolate may come from the cacao tree, but where does the cacao tree come from? The cacao tree is native to the tropical rain forests of South and Central America. Tropical rain forests have four layers, each with its own kinds of plants and animals.

The Emergent Layer contains the tops of the very tallest trees (100- to 240-feet high) that peek out above the shorter trees of the canopy. This layer is home to birds, bats, and butterflies.

The Canopy is a leafy environment, containing the leaves and branches of many trees. Nearly 90 percent of all rain forest life is found here, including monkeys, reptiles, more insects, and plants such as mosses, vines, and orchids.

The Understory is a shady, humid layer with little plant and animal life. Below the canopy, but still above the forest floor, most of the plants and animals here don't need much light, such as beetles, small mammals, snakes, palms, ferns, and everyone's favorite, the cacao tree!

The Forest Floor is home to both the largest and smallest animals in the rain forest: Insects and spiders coexist with giant anteaters and jaguars! Plants don't often grow here because less than 1 percent of sunlight can penetrate the leafy plants in the layers above it.

And there you have it: the many layers of the tropical rain forest. Which layer would you most like to visit?

Foods from the Americas that Changed the World

Chocolate isn't the only food that European explorers brought back from the New World. Check out these familiar flavors, fruits, veggies, and other foods native to Mexico and South America.

 Corn – Mexico – Scientists believe that at least 7,000 years ago, Native Americans living in present day Mexico began cultivating corn, or maize, from a grass called teosinte. Today corn has become the most abundant grain crop in the world.

Vanilla – Mexico – Vanilla comes from the vanilla orchid, a plant native to the tropical rain forests of southeastern Mexico and Central America. The Aztecs believed it had medicinal properties and often added it to their hot chocolate!

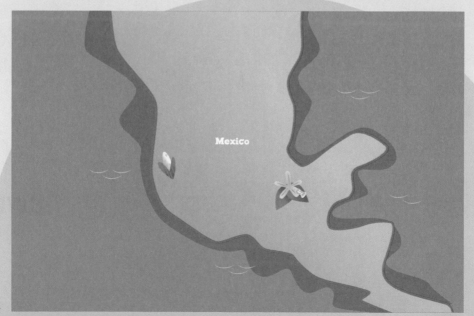

Mexico

Peanuts – Bolivia/Paraguay/Brazil –

Peanuts may be popular in dishes throughout Asia, but they actually come from South America! European explorers brought peanuts to Europe in the early 1500s.

Potatoes – Peru –

We might associate potatoes with Ireland, but these tasty spuds got their start in Peru, where the Incans first cultivated them.

Pineapples – Paraguay/Southern Brazil –

Native people in what is now Paraguay and southern Brazil traded pineapples throughout South America and the Caribbean, where Christopher Columbus tasted them in 1493. Columbus brought the fruit to Europe, where it quickly became popular for its sweet flavor.

Tomatoes – Chile/Bolivia/Ecuador/Peru –

I say "tomato," you say "Italy!" But tomatoes actually come from the Andes Mountains in South America, and for many years, Europeans thought they were poisonous!

How many of these foods have you tried?

Money Around the World

At one time, cacao beans were traded for goods, but what other things did people around the world once use for money?

Livestock – Believe it or not, many historians consider livestock such as cows, sheep, and camels to be the first form of money in the ancient world. Can you imagine what it would be like to pay for a new video game with sheep instead of dollars?

Cowrie Shells - The Chinese once used cowrie shells for money as early as 1500 B.C. Cowrie shells came from islands in the Pacific and Indian Oceans. They became popular as currency because they were small and easy to carry. The cowrie shell was eventually handled by many people around the world and has been used for longer and by more people than any other form of money.

Tools - In northern China cowrie shells were generally rare, so different coins shaped like small knives, hoes, and spades became popular as far back as 1000 B.C. Why shape them like tools? Farming played a big role in ancient China, and everyone knew the value of these tools in their day-to-day work!

Wampum - Many Native American tribes as well as early European settlers used wampum, or beads made from small clam shells. The beads were strung on a cord and were sometimes worn as belts or necklaces. Wampum became a powerful force in early America—the oldest corporation in North America, Hudson's Bay Company, had a profitable bead-trading market with the Native Americans.

Being an expert on something means you can get an awesome score on a quiz on that subject! Take this

HISTORY OF HOT CHOCOLATE QUIZ

to see how much you've learned.

1. Hot chocolate is made using the beans of what tree?

a. Papaya
b. Cacao
c. Peach

2. The _____ people of Central America started growing cacao 3,500 years ago.

a. Olmec
b. Chinese
c. Appalachian

3. When did Hernán Cortés first bring hot chocolate to the Spanish court?

a. 1830s
b. 1240s
c. 1520s

4. What Caribbean island did the British conquer, allowing them to grow cacao?

a. Jamaica
b. Cuba
c. Grenada

5. Thomas Jefferson thought that hot chocolate would become more popular than ___ or ___.

a. Cookies, Cake
b. Tea, Coffee
c. Ham, Eggs

6. When was chocolate first produced as a solid food?

a. 2006
b. 1692
c. 1847

7. Milton Hershey bought a chocolate-manufacturing machine at the ___ World's Fair in 1893.

a. Chicago
b. Moscow
c. San Francisco

8. Explorer Roald Amundsen took hot chocolate with him on his 1911 expedition to where?

a. The North Pole
b. The South Pole
c. Mount Everest

9. Hot cocoa is included in modern military cuisine as part of soldiers' _____.

a. BLTs
b. SATs
c. MREs

48

Answers: 1.b 2.a 3.c 4.a 5.b 6.c 7.a 8.b 9.c